HOW ADHD AFFECTS HOME ORGANIZATION

Understanding the Role of the 8 Key Executive Functions of the Mind

BY

LISA WOODRUFF

ISBN-13: 978-1545589007
ISBN-10: 1545589003

This book is dedicated to all those who have helped me grow in my knowledge and understanding of ADHD and how it affects every aspect of a person's life.

To Springer School and Center in Cincinnati for their continued pursuit of knowledge, best practices, and strategies that benefit both the students at the school and the Cincinnati community at large in the fields of learning disabilities and ADHD.

To The Affinity Center for their Multidisciplinary Assessment and Treatment approach to treating ADHD at all ages with a unique holistic view.

I am thoroughly fascinated by the way the mind works. It is my desire that at the end of this book, you too will understand how the ADHD mind can learn to be organized.

TABLE OF CONTENTS

FOREWORD

Lisa Woodruff has a natural affinity for jigsaw puzzles—she actually *enjoys* working with all those pesky little scattered pieces to make them fit together. I don't get it. (Jigsaw puzzles make me queasy.) Despite her great fortune in having an aptitude for envisioning order when she sees chaos and for organizing just about anything while actually enjoying the process, Lisa is still quite a likeable person.

Lisa understands at its core, as only a few do, the anguish and shame experienced—particularly by many women with ADHD—when disorganization overwhelms a person's life. Women with ADHD often move through life accompanied by an unending stream of "should" messages running through the backs of their minds. "I should be able to keep up with the laundry" or "I should be able to organize the house and keep it that way," for example. When other people seem to be able to do these things with relative ease, those with ADHD struggle with the belief beneath all those "should" messages: "something must be wrong with me."

Fortunately, Lisa knows better. She knows why organization can be so challenging. And she knows with certainty that it's not because something is wrong with you. She knows the ways in which specific aspects of attention functioning (also called executive functions) get in the way of organization. And she knows that "people resources" matter. She wants to help you learn the actual reasons why you struggle with organization. Lisa's deepest desire is to share with you the information and tools she's discovered that work for people with ADHD. There isn't a one-size-fits-all answer. But knowledge about ADHD and the executive functions leads directly to understanding what strategies can work for you, what strategies probably won't work for you, and why.

Lisa's wisdom, humor, and perspective are quite unique and powerful. The same is true of the wisdom, humor, and perspective you'll find in these pages. You're in good hands.

Chris Mayhall, PhD

INTRODUCTION

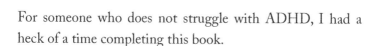

For someone who does not struggle with ADHD, I had a heck of a time completing this book.

Here's why.

ADHD is a complex spectrum disorder. I am a wife, mom, and professional organizer.

I knew how to help get a home organized, but I struggled against my own fears of offending others, not having perfect information, and not having a one-size-fits-all solution for you to implement and follow in three easy steps after reading this book.

I was making this way too hard.

Let me start at the beginning.

Too often, when women call Organize 365 to ask us to help them get organized, they end up whispering to me, "Um, well… I have ADHD," or "I'm depressed," or "I can't stay focused."

Women feel like they are broken if they can't do this organization thing on their own. And that grieves me.

Organization is a skill that can be learned by anyone at any time. I truly believe that. It's just easier for some than for others.

While I myself do not have ADHD, I have successfully parented, taught, and professionally organized those who do.

And along the way, I learned a lot about how the brain works.

One of the best emails I ever received said, "Oh, my gosh! No one has ever been able to explain my brain to me before! You know how I think!"

Others email me in tears, saying now they understand why they haven't been able to make the progress that they wanted to make in organizing their homes.

Knowledge is power.

So I must share what I know.

Even if it only helps one person.

That person might be you.

Lisa

HOW TO READ THIS BOOK

If you are reading this book, it is likely that you have been diagnosed with, or suspect you have, ADHD.

Here's what I know about you.

You think *fast*.

You don't need rosy explanations or lots of extra words. They just bog you down.

Get to the point.

Okay, I will.

In Part 1 of this book, I will address a whole host of related topics that usually come up with my ADHD clients.

Each of these topics are addressed in super-short chapters, so you can easily skim through them and read only those that interest or apply to you.

In Part 2, I will dive into each of the six executive functions that I have helped clients and students overcome to live more organized lives.

At the end of each chapter, you'll find a list of related Organize 365 podcast episodes to help you delve deeper into that topic.

When you see this symbol: , go to organize365.com/ADHDbook to see pictures of the organization ideas mentioned, links to additional blog posts and podcasts, and links to other electronic resources.

And finally, in Part 3, I will provide some additional resources to help you move forward in getting your home organized!

Let's get started.

Part 1

ADHD AND THE 8 EXECUTIVE FUNCTIONS

WHAT ADHD IS AND ISN'T – LET'S GET ON THE SAME PAGE

In this book, I will share with you my experience and research about ADHD and how it relates to home organization. It stands to reason that we should start by defining terms.

ADHD is a spectrum disorder that manifests itself through the 8 executive processes of the brain: flexible thinking, working memory, self-monitoring, task initiation, planning, organization, impulse control, and emotional control.

Basically, the executive functions of the brain help you plan, organize, and complete tasks.

The term "spectrum disorder" means that which executive functions are impacted and to what degree varies from one person to another.

While you may have a deficit in one area and be strong in the other seven, another person with the same diagnosis may have a deficit in seven areas and be strong in only one.

Additionally, there are indications your executive function does not reach maturity until the age of thirty. The brain is an amazing and dynamic organ.

This is important because understanding which executive functions you struggle with will help you decide which strategies and accommodations to implement to finally get your house organized!

THE 8 EXECUTIVE FUNCTIONS OF THE BRAIN DEFINED

So what are the 8 executive functions of the mind?

1. **Flexible Thinking.** The ability to adjust to the unexpected. Someone who struggles with flexible thinking has a hard time when someone else changes their schedule at the last minute.
2. **Working Memory.** The ability to keep multiple pieces of information in your mind at the same time. Someone who struggles with working memory easily forgets what they are saying in a conversation and misses steps in multistep directions.
3. **Self-Monitoring.** The ability to evaluate what you're doing compared to other people. Someone who struggles with self-monitoring can have an overly positive or overly negative view of themselves.
4. **Task Initiation.** The ability to take action and get started. Someone who struggles with task initiation knows what to do, but cannot make themselves do it.
5. **Planning.** The ability to pick out what the most important thing is to do next in order to get everything done. Someone who struggles with planning resists making lists

because they are overwhelmed with everything that needs to be done. They cannot prioritize the weight of one activity over the next and default to taking care of things when they reach a critical state.

6. **Organization**. The ability to keep track of things mentally and physically. Someone who struggles with organization has a hard time putting items away and remembering where they left items when they are not put away.

7. **Impulse Control**. The ability to think before acting. Someone who struggles with impulse control will blurt out a statement and wish they could take it back or impulsively eat a cookie before remembering they are on a diet.

8. **Emotional Control**. The ability to keep your feelings in check. Someone who struggles with emotional control can take suggestions as criticism and overreact.

I am *not* going to cover these last two executive functions in this book.

The executive functions of impulse control and emotional control tend to have the least impact on the adults I work with, in my opinion.

Impulse control involves thinking before acting. In home organization, I don't see this as a significant area of concern.

Emotional control is the ability to keep emotions in check. While I am sure this does impact people's abilities to organize their homes, this is beyond my pay grade to explain in this book. ☺

Do you learn better by listening to audio? *This book is available on Audible. You can get your copy at a reduced rate if you bought this book on Amazon.*

WHAT IF YOU HAVE MORE THAN ONE DIAGNOSIS? YOU HAVE ADHD AND...

These are co-morbid diagnoses of ADHD.

I know it sounds terrible, but that is the medical term that is used when you have more than one diagnosis at a time and they're related to each other.

Here's how I explain it. Let's take, for example, diabetes and asthma. Obviously, those two are very distinct diagnoses, right? If you have *both* of those, you have two diagnoses, not one. As far as I know, there is not an overlap in symptoms or disposition to have those two diagnoses together.

The National Institute on Drug Abuse defines co-morbidity this way, "When two disorders or illnesses occur in the same person, simultaneously or sequentially, they are described as co-morbid. Co-morbidity also implies interactions between the illnesses that affect the course and prognosis of both."

With ADHD, there are many diagnoses where there are similar symptoms like anxiety, depression, learning disabilities,

OCD, etc. On average, 50 percent or more of people diagnosed with ADHD will also have a co-morbid diagnosis.

This is important to know because in my experience, the addition of multiple diagnoses actually multiplies the symptoms experienced.

Let's put it this way. If you have mild ADHD and that is your only diagnosis, learning a few strategies and adaptations will significantly improve your ability to organize.

However, if you have ADHD that impacts 7 of the 8 executive functions of your brain and the co-morbid diagnoses of anxiety and learning disabilities, that's a whole new ball game!

Working with a licensed therapist can help you see the strengths and weaknesses of each of your diagnoses so you can determine how to make the most progress.

ARE YOU A PERFECTIONIST?

While I have not done research on the interaction between perfectionism and ADHD, I have witnessed it many times. Perfectionism appears to exacerbate the executive functioning deficits that are already there. As a general rule, if I have two clients with the same ADHD symptoms and one is a perfectionist, it is going to be monumentally harder for the perfectionist to get organized.

The idea that there is a "perfect" solution, or the desire for a guarantee that each strategy will work before we start implementing, often leads to never starting.

Organization is a journey, *not* a destination. Most people are not "born organized." It is a skill that can be learned, and I would love to teach it to you!

If you have perfectionist tendencies, I want you to embrace this new journey. I promise to be kind and help you every step of the way.

It's not going to be perfect, but getting started will be better than the imperfect mess you have now.

I preach "progress, not perfection."

Perfectionistic thinking will be addressed in the chapter about the executive function of task initiation (also known as getting started). This is a biggie—it's probably the number one reason I see for why people are not organized.

And it's not surprising at all when you consider that the executive function of task initiation can be impaired not only by ADHD, but also by anxiety, depression, bipolar disorder, and perfectionism.

THREE TIPS THAT ALMOST ALWAYS WORK

Here are the three tips I have found that consistently help my students and clients with ADHD:

#1 Using people resources keeps you focused

This is why a professional organizer helps you get organized. Not only do they come in and organize your house lickety-split for you, but in many cases, having the professional organizer there keeps you focused.

We keep you focused, we keep you moving, we task-switch you when you get stuck on something, and we know how to move you on to the next thing. Accomplishing all of that would be very, very hard—if not impossible—to do on your own. Of course, not everyone can hire a professional organizer, but when you do have the resources, they are well spent!

#2 Create structure and... it!

A lot of women call Organize 365 in their mid-30s. They were able to function through their school years, early parenthood, and their first jobs.

But then life got going too fast, and the lack of the daily structure of the school day or the babies' nap schedules left them at a loss as to how to use their time well.

It happens all the time. Your parents provided the structure for you. You got up, you went to school. You were in sports, you had sports calendars. And you just kept going from thing to thing, where people were directing you what to do.

And then you had a baby. The baby had a nap time, and then the baby had playdates, and then preschool. You had structure.

Whether the structure is imposed by somebody else or self-imposed, you need structure to get through your day.

One structure I have set up for you is the Sunday Basket. If you were struggling for years and years with your daily actionable paper and now you've implemented the Sunday Basket and it's working, it's because I have created a structure for you. This is where mail goes. This is how often we go through it. This is exactly how we go through it. This is what we get rid of. And then we do it again next week. The Sunday Basket process is very, very structured.

If this is the first time you're hearing about the Sunday Basket, don't worry. We'll get to it in Part 3.

#3 Less stuff helps.

I know you're saying, "No kidding, Lisa. Why do you think I'm reading this book? I don't know how to get rid of this stuff, but I understand I would be doing better if there was less stuff here."

Good! We are on the same page. ☺ I promise, you will enjoy knowing where your stuff is more than keeping it all.

Let's move on to Part 2: How Each Executive Function Affects Home Organization.

Related Organize 365 podcast episodes

- Episode 144 – How to Get Organized in 3 Easy Steps, Step 1: Declutter
- Episodes, 156, 157, 159, 160 – The Declutter Madness Series for the Whole Family

Part 2

HOW EACH EXECUTIVE FUNCTION AFFECTS HOME ORGANIZATION

EXECUTIVE FUNCTION #1: FLEXIBLE THINKING

What is the executive function of flexible thinking?

Flexible thinking allows you to move freely from one situation to another and to adjust in order to respond appropriately to each situation.

In other words, to go with the flow.

Flexible thinking is impacted by both ADHD and anxiety. It's not uncommon for people with either diagnosis to have a rigid "my way or the highway" response to change. It is my experience that this is often a reaction to the loss of control.

Think about a time when you had your day all planned out and then… you got a flat tire, your child got sick, your friend stopped by unexpectedly. What just flashed through your mind?

Were you excited?

Frustrated?

For how long?

There is no "perfect amount of flexibility." Flexible thinking is all about how easily you can pivot and deal with the unexpected that life throws at you every day.

In addition to helping you adjust to day-to-day changes in your schedule, flexible thinking affects how you view spaces in your home and what labels you put on different types of containers.

Here is why you need flexible thinking to get your home organized.

When you have strong flexible thinking, it means that you can adjust to the unexpected.

You roll with the punches.

You can go with the flow.

You can pivot.

If you do not have flexible thinking, you're very rigid. You want to have a very structured day; you don't like when unexpected things happen. One minor thing can happen in the morning and your entire day will be off.

Now obviously, no one is completely flexible or completely rigid. This is a spectrum too, right?

I am pretty flexible and I can think outside of the box, I can come up with solutions. But when unexpected things happen, it does knock me off my game for a couple of minutes.

If a bunch of unexpected events happen in a row, then maybe it will derail half my day. Sometimes it will derail my whole day. Everyone has a threshold of how many things can come at them unexpectedly without throwing them completely off course.

Here is a great example of what I see happen 99 percent of the time when I come in as a professional organizer to work with a client who does not have flexible thinking.

They have tried organization and it has not worked.

They think: "Okay, I'm ready to get organized." In their minds, "get organized" equals:

- Go to Target and go to the section where they sell organizational supplies.
- Pick out a whole lot of plastic containers with lids, in whatever color I like.
- Spend a couple hundred dollars on those.
- Bring those home to whatever area of the house is "unorganized."
- Put all of my stuff into these beautiful containers.
- Put the containers on the shelves.
- Put a picture on Facebook.
- I'm organized.

Organization = Containers = "Pinterest like."

Then what happens is, it doesn't work for them.

- They can't remember what they put in the boxes.
- They can't remember to put stuff back in the boxes.
- They go buy more stuff because they forgot what box they put it in.
- They didn't buy clear boxes and they can't see what's in there.

So they resign themselves to failure. "Great, I tried that whole organizational thing. I spent a good $200 and three days of my life to organize my pantry. Then I had to go buy a bunch of new food, because by the time I found where I had put my old food, it was all expired."

You might be laughing and you might be thinking: "Bingo. That's me. And that's why I hate organization and I can't be organized."

Not true.

Organization has nothing to do with containers. You've just been sold that bill of goods.

Often, if you don't have flexible thinking, what you think is that this one solution solves this one problem, and if it didn't work for me, that problem can't be solved for me.

Somebody with flexible thinking is able to see more than one solution to your problem.

Problem: You want your pantry to look like Pinterest. You are tired of seeing empty boxes that have no cereal bars in them. You think you have cereal bars for the kids. You get up in the morning, you go to the box, it's empty. Kids have no cereal bars, you're frustrated, somebody has to organize this pantry. Right?

Solution: I hang over-the-door shoe pockets on the back of my client's pantry doors. I cut them in half so they only cover the bottom of the door and hang them with Command Hooks. Then you can actually see all the different kinds of cereal bars and protein bars and protein shake mixes that you have at one time.

The pockets are little enough that 5 to 10 bars will fit in each pocket. It's low enough that the kids can get their own snacks. It's easy enough that the whole family can follow the pattern that you've set out. And then when you plan to go to the grocery store, you can look and see which cereal bars are most popular and which ones you need to buy again.

This system works really well when you're on a new diet and you're trying all these different flavors of protein bars. You can have all the different flavors in different pockets and easily see at the end of the week which one everybody in the family liked most, because that's the pocket that's empty.

Different solutions for different problems.

Organization is done in incremental stages.

If you went and bought a hundred dollars' worth of beautiful plastic containers for your pantry, it probably worked for at least 50 percent of your foods. The bins for rices and starches may be working great.

Next, you tried the cereal bars organizer on the door and that is actually working. But you haven't found a good solution for the cereal.

Now you are in organization level two, where the flexible thinking is hard.

Problem: What is another way I could organize cereal? Emptying all the cereal into expensive Tupperware containers with lids didn't work because the kids didn't put the lids on correctly and all the cereal went bad. (Guess how I know this doesn't work.)

Solution: What I've started doing with all of the clients that I organize is to just take all the bagged cereal out of the box. Then, we put a chip clip on the bag and put all the bags of cereal in a basket.

All cereal comes in a clear bag inside its box. When you pull that bag out of the box, you can see exactly what kind of cereal it is through the bag. It works with Pops Cereal and Apple Chex and all of them. They all look different and they're all in clear bags. This works fabulously. It takes up less space than those expensive containers do, and you can just roll the bags down tighter and the cereal stays pretty fresh.

Now we've solved your cereal problem. There's only one problem with this solution for cereal: What if you buy both Honey Nut and regular Cheerios? They look the same without the cardboard packaging. So you actually need to take a Sharpie marker and write on the bags which is which. Other than that, this has worked for everyone that I have organized cereal for in the last five years.

Now if you really struggle with flexible thinking, what's going to happen is that because you don't understand these different systems, you are thinking, well, okay, great. You told me where to put cereal bars, and you told me where to put starches and cereal. But you didn't tell me where to put tomato soup. And because you don't have flexible thinking, you don't know what to do with your soup. I didn't even mention a canned item. What do you do with canned soups?

(Don't worry, I won't leave you hanging. Go to organize365. com/ADHDbook to see a picture of the organization ideas mentioned above, as well as how I store cans on shoe organizers!)

This is why flexible thinking really impacts your organization skills. You do have to be kind of flexible when you're organizing. Try different things. Keep what is working and try different solutions for what is not.

Match the container to the stuff.

Here's another example of flexible thinking. I was organizing my nightstand drawer. And my nightstand drawer has office supplies in it because I sit on my bed and do my work at night.

Problem: I had bought different drawer organizers for my nightstand drawer in the past, but they weren't working for the items I was currently storing. The traditional desk-drawer-organizer storage compartments were too square. I needed thin rectangles.

I went and bought a few drawer organizers, and I brought them home. They didn't work at all.

Solution: I went back to the store. I went up and down every single aisle, looking at every single organizer that would fit in that drawer, thinking about the things that I had to organize.

- A 7-day-a-week pill container
- Pens and pencils
- Nail polish supplies
- Chap Stick
- Mints
- TV remotes

I looked all over the store… in the bathroom supply aisles and the kitchen supply section, not just the office supply area. Anything that was plastic and would fit in that drawer, I looked at.

What I ended up coming home with was an acrylic utensil holder that you would put in your kitchen to organize your silverware drawer. And to be honest, I would not buy this one for the kitchen because unless you only have four spoons, it wouldn't be big enough. But it was perfect for my nightstand drawer.

Action steps for improving your flexible thinking as it relates to home organization:

1. **Listen to the Organize 365 Podcast.** Listening to the Organize 365 Podcast will help you with flexible thinking because I'm always telling you these out-of-the-box ideas I have about organizing. It will give you a bigger bank to draw from as you go to organize different areas of your home. It will grow your mental library of alternative organization solutions for each space in your house.

2. **Go on Pinterest to find organization solutions.** Once you know what you want to organize, go look at all the different ways people have organized that item or space. Pinterest is a great resource for you if you really struggle with flexible thinking, because it will give you a bank of ideas to draw from as you go to organize different spaces.

3. **Check out pictures associated with the ideas in this book at organize365.com/ADHDbook.**

Executive Function #2: Working Memory

What is the executive function of working memory?

Working memory is the capacity to hold information in the mind for the purpose of completing a task.

"Multitasking," you may think.

No, not really, but kinda.

Research has shown that no one can actually multitask. What multitaskers do is rapidly task-switch.

Following multistep directions or completing math word problems is challenging if you struggle with working memory.

Here is how working memory helps you get your home organized.

You walk into a space that needs to be organized and all the disorder is overwhelming. Each individual item in the room yells out to you "Organize me!" and it is deafening.

You reach out to silence the stray socks, and the open chip bag catches your eye.

Once the bag is sealed, you see a bill you meant to mail and go to grab it.

But what do you let go of? The stray socks or the chips you *just* bought that are about to go bad *again*?!

Now you are out of hands, overwhelmed, and defeated.

It's been 30 seconds.

Oh well, maybe your friend wants to go for coffee. At least the coffee shop is organized.

And out the door you go.

Working memory is the part of your brain that is able to hold multiple things in the forefront of your thoughts so you can synthesize them into a new idea.

I am a visual person. When I'm organizing with people, it's like I'm putting together this gigantic jigsaw puzzle. And I love to do jigsaw puzzles.

When I go into a room, my mind takes a picture of that room. And if I walk out of that room, I can describe everything in it in detail.

I remember the first time that I realized that I did this and many people didn't. I was organizing a garage with a client.

She found a pink shoe and asked, "Do we have another pink shoe?"

And I said, "It's behind me to the left, two feet."

She exclaimed, "How do you do that?"

And I said, "Oh, you don't do that?" It was just logical to me. I had scanned the room and taken a mental picture of everything in it. Then as I found things, I was able to match them with other things that were in the room. It's just how I think.

I can literally start in the corner of one room and go all the way around the room clockwise and organize it like that. If you have a hard time with working memory, you wouldn't make it through 10 percent of the room this way. It would be information overload.

Problem: Your own clutter distracts you and overwhelms you before you can make any progress organizing a room.

Solution: Walk into the room with a mission to do one thing—and only one thing.

Session 1: The very first thing you're going to do is find everything that's trash.

Take a trash bag and talk to yourself, chanting, "Trash, trash, trash."

By chanting, "Trash, trash, trash," you will keep your mind from wandering and thinking, "Oh, I wonder what that article is about." Or, "Oh, why didn't we return that?" Or, "Oh, I wonder what's on the TV."

You start to drift. But I don't want you to drift. I want you to organize this room.

When you are chanting, "Trash, trash, trash," even if your mind starts to wander, your mouth is saying, "Trash, trash, trash" and it snaps you out of it. You think, "Oh yeah, trash! I'm finding trash. I'm supposed to be finding trash."

When you think that you don't have any more trash in that room, take one more look around the room and you'll probably find more.

The first time through, you are going to see the obvious trash. The second time through, you'll think, "Oh, I didn't see that." It's like you've developed a blindness to it.

Just keep going until you literally cannot find another single thing in that room that's trash. Then tie up the bag; you're done for the day. Okay? You've done a great job.

Session 2: Now, the next time you come in, you're going to chant, "Food and dishes, food and dishes, food and dishes."

Maybe your kids left the chip bag and their plates in the family room. Go ahead and collect all the plates and take them to the sink. Collect all the food and put it away. Go back. Okay, any more plates? Any more food? And I often will say, any more trash? Because if it's been a day, there's probably new trash, right?

Session 3: On the third time through the same space, I focus on clothing items. I will walk around the room, or walk around my house, and I will say, "Clothing, clothing, I'm picking up clothing," and I take it right into the laundry room.

Now you've gotten the obvious out: the trash, the dishes, the clothes. Now it's time to think, okay, what is my goal for this room? That's when you start going through the 15minuteaday organizing tasks.

If you have trouble with working memory, you don't start on 15minute daily organizing tasks until you've done the day of trash, the day of dishes, and the day of clothing. Or maybe you've done trash, dishes, and clothing in one fell swoop and you are ready to move on.

Some examples of 15minute daily organizing tasks are:

- Go through all the VHS tapes.
- Find all the games that don't have pieces that go with them.
- Look at all your suitcases.

In my program, I encourage you to really narrow in on one thing. I tell you what to eliminate. I tell you how to organize it, and then I tell you to move on. That's why an organization program is great if you struggle with ADHD: it will help you laser in on one single little area.

Essentially, what you're doing with your working memory is you are chunking tasks.

Chunking tasks means breaking down big projects into manageable pieces. This makes it easier to get through the process of organizing.

The concept of chunking tasks originated in the field of cognitive psychology. As a teacher, I used this concept to break down texts and assignments into smaller chunks to help my students process, understand, and remember them better.

As a professional organizer, I apply the same concept with my clients in their homes. Instead of saying, "Organize the kitchen," I direct you to organize the silverware drawer. The next day, I tell you to organize all the utensils. Finally, on the third day, we tackle the rest of the drawers.

Chunking tasks means breaking down the process of organizing into systematic steps that cumulatively lead to you getting all your drawers organized without getting distracted or overwhelmed.

The example above comes from my 15-minute-a-day program: The Productive Home Solution™. It is a paid program that walks you step by step through organizing your whole house in 15-minute increments every single day. (You can read more about this program in Part 3.)

The last thing I want to say about this:

If you struggle with working memory, write everything down. I jot down notes all the time: when I hear of a new book I want to read, think of something I want to tell you on the podcast—I write it all out. And I drop those notes in the Sunday Basket until Sunday. (You can read about the Sunday Basket in Part 3.)

Action steps for improving your working memory as it relates to home organization:

1. **Focus.** Your mind won't help you. You need to override it. Organize each room in this order:

   • Enter the space and *only* collect trash. Once *all* the trash is gone, go to step 2. (When I do this, I mutter under my breath "Trash, trash, trash" to keep me focused.)

   • Enter the space and *only* look for food. Rotten food, food that needs to be put away, and dishes food was or is on.

   • Enter the space and *only* look for clothes. Dirty clothes, new clothes, clothes you cleaned that didn't get put away.

   • Next, pick *one* type of item and collect *all* of those items before moving on.

2. **Use the Sunday Basket to leave yourself notes.** Empty your mind out on paper so you can focus on the task

44

at hand. Keep all of these notes in one location and go through them every Sunday so you don't miss important events or ideas.

3. **Find a 15minuteaday organization program** to help focus you on taking the next step in your organization journey every day.

Related Organize 365 podcast episodes

• Organization 101 (The Sunday Basket)

Executive Function #3: Self-Monitoring

What is the executive function of self-monitoring?

Self-monitoring is the ability to monitor one's own performance and to measure it against some standard of what is needed or expected.

Don't skip over this one.

Yes, I know you.

Self-monitoring is key to keeping you focused and motivated. When you can self-monitor, you can see how far you have come and be less overwhelmed by how far you need to go.

See, it's important!

This is a big one for perfectionists as well. Watch the standard to which you are comparing yourself. I often say I am a functional organizer, not a Pinterest organizer. My solutions work, but they don't usually end up in magazines.

Focus on getting organized, not on becoming Martha Stewart.

This is also why you see very few DIY projects at Organize 365. My focus is getting you organized, not creating organizational projects and works of art.

Of course, you can do all that and take your organization to the next level... just get the first level of organization done first!

Here is why you need to self-monitor to get your home organized.

Self-monitoring, as it applies to home organization, is the ability to see how far you've come and not lose track of time. This is why in the Organize 365 Facebook group, I'm always saying, "Give me the before and after pictures."

Give me the before and after pictures of the space you are organizing every day, or even every week. It's not for me, although I do love to see it. It's for you.

Learn to recognize your progress not just perfection.

Problem: As you start to get organized, you have a hard time seeing the progress you have made and estimating how long tasks will take.

Self-monitoring is one of the main things professional organizers help with when working with a client. At the beginning of the session, clients will typically be very nervous to have us there, very embarrassed. But they start anyway because they think, "I just can't live this way anymore. Fine. Just come in and help me," and we get started. They also tend to be excited: "Okay, the professionals are here. It's all going to get fixed."

When we get started, they have a lot of energy. Then somewhere between hours two and three, I can just see it come over their faces. "Oh, my gosh. We're not going to get done in one day. This is never going to end. It's going to cost a fortune. I can't make any more decisions. I don't know what to do." It's like when you know your kid is ready for a nap, and you can just see them melting down right in front of you.

This is exactly what happens with my clients. Our whole team knows: "Okay, they hit the wall. This is time." We start offering more encouragement and saying, "Look at how far we've come. Look at how much we've done. Look at how many bags are full that we're donating."

Since we keep the client right with us in the thick of it, pushing her to keep making decisions and keep going, we may have finished one room and moved on to a second by now. But the client isn't seeing the completed room, because we are keeping her with us while we are working to get the job done.

Solution: At this point, our team keeps working in the rooms that are not organized and we move the client back to the room that is organized.

We get up, we walk into that room, and we say, "You remember what this looked like at the beginning? Look… Your kids' playroom is totally done and they could play in the playroom. Isn't this going to be great when they come home?"

The fresh perspective washes over the client, and she says, "Oh, yeah. I can't believe we did that."

"Look, here are all the bags that we filled and that are going to be gone."

And she remembers. "Oh, okay. This is great."

Now, depending on the client and depending on her emotional control and impulse control, maybe that's all she needed. She takes a deep breath. She gets her favorite beverage. Sometimes it's alcoholic early in the morning. We don't care. We take her back into the unorganized spaces with us to keep going.

Sometimes she's done.

I would say that by the time you get to two and a half hours (our sessions go five hours), with four out of every ten clients, they're done, done. You're not getting any more out of them, I don't care if you use a defibrillator. They are done organizing for the day. In that case, we tell them to go shopping, go to lunch, go watch TV, go work from home on their computer, whatever. We keep going because we can organize with or without the client.

The ability to see how far you've come and to give yourself the energy to go forward will really come into play in the next chapter about task initiation.

How do you get yourself organized without a professional organizer?

Problem: The majority of us will not have the resources or the availability of a professional organizer to help us get organized. So how do you help yourself self-monitor?

Solution #1: Join a free Facebook group. Being around like-minded people all working on the same goals will help you stay focused and get more ideas.

However, be careful not to compare your organizing efforts with someone else's. Use the group to post your before and after pictures. Looking at only the after pictures will not help you see how far you have come.

I'd love for you to join the Organize 365 Facebook group. Use this link: organize365.com/Facebook.

Solution #2: Get an organizing buddy.

Find a friend with similar goals, and encourage and motivate each other to make daily progress in organizing your homes. The best scenario would be for you both to organize the same spaces in your homes at the same time so you can share even more ideas.

Don't forget to take the before pictures!

Solution #3: Join an online organizing program with a group-coaching component.

For many people, this is the best solution, and it comes at a fraction of the cost of an in-home professional organizer. A good program will help you to systematically organize a space one day at a time. As you progress through the program, each area will get—and—stay organized as you move on to the next one.

Take full advantage of any forums, Facebook groups, or Q&A sessions the leader provides to get feedback and share your progress.

Organizing your home is a large undertaking. It is not a task you can do in spurts, or even just a few days a week. Cumulative daily action is the key. Over time, that's what will yield an organized home.

Action steps for improving your self-monitoring as it relates to home organization:

1. **Post before and after pictures in an online community** (like the Organize 365 Community - organize365.com/app).

   You will be amazed by how many suggestions you can get when you are stuck—and by the encouragement and praise you will get for each accomplishment.

Honestly, the community aspect will get you going and keep you going.

And the best part... you will inspire others to share and give them ideas, too!

2. **Find a friend.** Partner with someone to hold you accountable and share the successes of each of your organizational victories.

3. **Join a home organization program.** Following a plan to get your home organized in a systematic order will yield quicker results.

Executive Function #4: Task Initiation

What is the executive function of task initiation (also known as getting started)?

Task initiation is the ability to begin a task or activity and to independently generate ideas, responses, or problem-solving strategies necessary to sustain the attention and focus levels needed to complete the task.

This applies to new tasks or tasks that we don't want to do. You may struggle with task initiation even though you have no problem starting and sustaining your attention on the projects you love to do.

All of us have at some time had to deal with the inability to get started on things, but for people who struggle with the executive function of task initiation, the challenges can be overwhelming. As a teacher, there were four skills I used to look at when I was helping a student—and they're the same skills that come into play with a client who has task-initiation difficulties. They are:

- the ability to start
- working memory
- focused attention
- energy regulation

The simplest example I can think of to show you all of these pieces in play—and strategies for dealing with them—is a child with ADHD trying to do a math worksheet. And while this has nothing to do with organizing your house, I am fairly certain you have at some point had to do a math worksheet you didn't want to do.

The ability to start

Few of my students loved math. So for many of them, they had to reach down deep and decide they were going to get the math done and do it now. My students with ADHD would just not start. The assignment would be late, they would "lose" it, and finally, I would sit down with them and they would decide they were going to get the math done.

But once a child and I were together at a desk, the real work of doing the worksheet was paralyzing.

Because I do not have ADHD, I can only imagine the feelings that were happening in that child, but here is what I have surmised over time. There is an overwhelming, almost panic-level physical event going on inside that child. It is not a case where they just want to blow off the work and go play.

They don't know how to do the work. And they want to do it perfectly. The page just seems so overwhelming. They feel like this will never end and they will be here forever doing yucky math.

Working memory

Working memory is the ability to follow multistep directions, keep multiple pieces of information in your head at the same time, and recall information out of your brain's filing cabinet as it's needed. In US classrooms, by the third grade, almost all math problems involve multistep directions and remembering rules from past lessons and past years.

So I would provide my ADHD students with a math resource sheet with all the formulas they needed to complete the worksheet. Providing this resource allowed each student to show me what they knew and whether they could apply what they had learned. I needed to make sure I was testing for the skill being taught and not penalizing a student for a poor working memory.

It took me a few years to really understand how much of struggle word retrieval and memory recall can be for some people. In today's iPhone age, using apps and resources to aid in memory recall will really help those with a low working memory.

Focused attention

Are you exhausted just reading about this? Imagine being our poor math student trapped with me at their desk. Okay: we are at the desk and we have the resources we need to do the worksheet. So just get it done, right?

Wrong.

Every single problem on that paper is a *new* task that needs to be initiated. Oh boy!

You can see it on our third grader's face. They get started, complete the problem, and then slump back in their chair.

There is a reason I am sitting at the desk. I see the slump coming and I say, "Next one" or "Keep going" or "Good job" or "Two more". Anything to distract them from their inner voice saying, "Great job, you did one. Now let's take a break."

A child gets help in focusing their attention from a parent or a teacher. As an adult, you'll need to look for a coach, friend, boss, spouse, or accountability partner to help you strengthen this muscle.

Energy regulation

Have you ever watched a third-grader with ADHD do math problems? They can be laughing with a friend one minute and a moment later, they look like a sad wet noodle poured into a school desk.

Getting the pencil in their hand ready to write (as opposed to being used a twirling stick) is a feat in and of itself. And then, once the problems are done, they are back up bouncing around the classroom full of energy.

What happened?

Again, I have not experienced this myself, so I cannot say 100% for sure, but my observation is that the task being presented can be so overwhelming that the body responds by shutting down. In some cases literally.

I have seen students curl up in a ball and remain motionless for over an hour because they cannot do the math work presented—no matter how many strategies I use.

If this is you, you may be thinking, "Yes! Yes, that's exactly how it feels."

If this is not you, you may think I am full of it and this is hogwash.

It's not.

I am not a medical doctor; I cannot explain it. But I can tell you it is real.

You need to find ways to manage energy regulation.

As a math teacher, I had to find a way to teach my students math. So I would try again the next day. Sometimes I varied the assignment. Sometimes I created something else for the student to show me they understood the concept. And sometimes we skipped it.

Task initiation is a muscle that you develop over time in each area of your life. It is harder when you have ADHD, but it is not impossible.

My third grade math students have grown up, and some of them even love math now. In most cases, it was not the math they disliked; it was learning how to augment their working memory and develop routines, systems, and strategies to make tasks that came easily for others achievable for them as well.

So let's bring this back to organizing your home.

Here is why you need to be able to initiate tasks to get your home organized.

If this is your struggle, you may like my blog and podcast, but you still *can't start*.

I know, frustrating!

My words make sense, but you aren't making progress. WHY?!

In most cases, it is because you have *too much* information.

I hear all the time about how my podcasts and posts are changing people's mindsets about getting organized. Maybe they have even had some successes, but with each new project, they really struggle to get started.

If this is you… you need information *as* you need it, not all at once.

Getting started on a project involves two things:

#1 Knowing how to do the project.

Listening to the Organize 365 podcast and reading this book are helping you learn how to organize your home. Since we are specifically talking about how to organize your home in this book, I am not going to expound on the *how* part of this executive function. Instead, let's focus on #2.

#2 Sustaining attention in order to finish the task.

That's not walking into the room to collect trash, finding a new magazine, sitting down, and reading the magazine. You got started, you got in the room, and then you got distracted.

Work on making incremental progress versus trying to go for the dream organization look (which by the way, I haven't been able to achieve yet, and I do this for a living).

Problem: You set unrealistic goals. "Okay, I want this to look like a Martha Stewart office. I have $25 and two hours." Probably not going to happen, right?

Solution: Instead of saying, "How do I get this entire office done perfectly?" can you walk in and say, "What is one thing I can do in this room today to make this office more organized?"

It may be locating all the pens and pencils, testing to see if they work, and putting them all in one drawer.

Another task may be collecting all the loose papers and putting them in a box.

If you are working on your filing cabinet, a task would be to go through one file folder. Discard or shred what you no longer need and relabel the file.

Finding one task to start and complete will give you a feeling of success and motivate you to take the next step. You are building your task-initiation muscle.

Setting your ideal time to do organization-related tasks

Problem: Mornings are super hard. I don't know very many people who've been diagnosed with ADHD and would consider themselves morning people.

Solution: Schedule your daily organization tasks in the evening hours or on the weekends. Organization is probably not a task you are super excited to get started on. So don't add it to the part of your day that is the hardest to get through.

Create a muscle memory for your organizing time.

Problem: Even if you're setting realistic goals and planning your organization tasks for the best times in your day, you *still* just can't seem to start.

Solution: Create a routine you go through each time you start an organizational task. Developing a muscle memory for your organizing time will break through some of the inertia you have around getting started.

Adam Dachis of *Lifehacker* defines muscle memory like this: "Muscle memory is not a memory stored in your muscles, of course, but memories stored in your brain that are much like a cache of frequently enacted tasks for your muscles. It's a form of procedural memory that can help you become very good at something through repetition."[1]

What do you do when you first wake up? For me, I go wake my son up, make his breakfast, brush my teeth, go to the bathroom, get in the shower, get dressed, wake my kids up again, dry my hair, check on my kids, do my make-up, let the dog out, start the coffee maker, get out the kids' medicines, pour their drinks, fix my coffee…

---

1   Adam Dachis, "How Muscle Memory Works and How It Affects Your Success," *Lifehacker* (blog), May 6, 2011, http://lifehacker.com/5799234/how-muscle-memory-works-and-how-it-affects-your-success.

The same way every day. When I alter the routine, that's when I forget things. But if I just go through my routine in the same order every day, it all gets done.

You can develop a muscle memory for your daily organizing time. In the beginning, you will need a checklist to follow as you train your brain to go through these steps, but over time, you will naturally go from one step to the next once you get started.

The more that you can create a routine, the more your body will start to play along and help you get started.

Here is a sample organizing routine:

1. Listen to the podcast or YouTube video about how to organize the space you want to organize.
2. Get all of your organizing supplies together for this project.
3. Walk into the selected room and start looking for trash as the podcast finishes.
4. Scan the room for any food, then laundry.
5. Start on the 15minute project of the day.

Even though you are adding 15–20 minutes to your total organizing time, this daily routine will get your mindset right, help you maintain your spaces (because you'll be picking up trash, food, and laundry each day), and create a routine that your body just follows each time you set out to "get organized," so the new 15minute daily task isn't so hard to start.

Figure out when your energy level is the highest for organizing. That time of day is your ideal time to use this routine. The more you use routine and consistency, the higher your chance of success will be.

Having too much information is a new home organizational problem.

Problem: You have too much information.

I think in the past, people sometimes didn't get started because they didn't know how to do something. Today, the exact opposite is true.

As a culture, we are leaving the Industrial Revolution and entering the Information Age. When I started blogging five years ago, the rule was to blog as much as you could. Get the content out there. Content is king. The idea was that if you wrote an article about organizing your bathroom, Google would be happy, and then when people searched "organizing your bathroom," your post would show up and you would get traffic.

That's not the case anymore. There is a new blog created every *six seconds*! There's too much information on how to organize your bathroom.

If you have a hard time getting started and you're a perfectionist, you're going to want to know the best way to get started. You will keep Googling and reading multiple professional organizers' ideas about how to organize bathrooms.

Each professional organizer is going to tell you how to organize a bathroom just a little bit differently. Then, you might go on Pinterest and think, "Ooh, I really like that bathroom by Moen," which is a faucet company. "That bathroom looks amazing. I'd love to have that bathroom." Mind you, that bathroom is like eight times the size of your bathroom. But nonetheless, that's the one that you want to have, because that's the one that you have pictured in your mind.

Next, you go to the website of a DIY blogger, not a professional organizing blogger, and she created a vanity out of a dead tree she had in her backyard. She chopped down the tree, cut it into planks, and assembled it into a beautiful vanity. "Wow," you think. "I want to create my own vanity, too. Wouldn't that be cool?"

At this point, you know what multiple professional organizers have to say. You've got these gorgeous "Better Homes and Gardens" pictures in your head of what your bathroom is going to look like from Moen, and then this Martha Stewart–type blogger has shown you how you can grow a tree and turn it into a... STOP!

You do nothing, because you have too much information.

Solution: Focus. Not just on organizing that space, but on one person's way of doing things.

Find someone you like. Start their program and finish it.

You can always follow another professional organizer, designer, or company later. But *get started* and *follow through* with one mentor at a time.

Finding one person to help you get through a project that's difficult for you will help you get started. If you keep going out there looking for more information, you'll be able to do that until you die. The amount of information available is never ending, and it's exponentially growing. At some point, you have to stop getting information and just get started.

Action steps for improving your task initiation as it relates to home organization:

1. **Adopt the mottos "Done is Better Than Perfect" and "Progress Over Perfection."** It really is a mindset shift. Do you want it perfect? Or do you want it better? Better is achievable.

2. **Figure out your ideal time of day.** Organization doesn't come naturally to you, so don't add in the layer of fighting your natural clock! Follow your energy flow.

3. **Follow one guru at a time.** It doesn't need to be me, but find one person who speaks to you and follow them. Buy

their books, join their free groups, read their free content, listen to their interviews, and do their program. Go all in. Committing is the first step.

Related Organize 365 podcast episodes

- Episode 81 – Where Do I Start Organizing?
- Episode 165 – The Power of When

EXECUTIVE FUNCTION #5: PLANNING

What is the executive function of planning?

Planning is the ability to manage current and future task demands.

In the last chapter, we focused on how to get started and follow through on tasks. In this chapter, we are looking at how you determine what you are following through on.

This is not the skill of starting a task and following through; this is the skill of knowing what task you need to do next. There are a lot of things you could do to get your house organized, but how do you choose? You may find yourself jumping from task to task instead of building on your past successes in a cumulative way to achieve a completely organized space.

Here is why you need to plan to get your home organized.

Planning is being able to see the big-picture goal (in this case, the organized house) and break that down into monthly, weekly, and daily tasks that achieve that goal.

The goal of organizing is not to do 15-minute-a-day random organizing projects. It is to do those daily organizational tasks in a focused way, leading to organized rooms—and, ultimately, an organized house.

Problem: You want your whole house organized.

One of my favorite questions to ask a potential home organization client in Cincinnati is when they would like us to have their house organized.

Can you guess what they say?

Yep—yesterday!

Even if you hire the pros, organization takes time. But it doesn't have to take forever.

Solution: Focus on one room to completion.

I always suggest that new readers or listeners start by making a Sunday Basket. This simple system typically takes about a weekend to make and 6–8 weeks to become a new habit. It is a quick win and shows you *can* get organized.

But where do you go from here?

Pick one room and focus on that room until it is organized. I suggest the kitchen. In my The Productive Home Solution™, the first 21 days focus on the kitchen.

Yes, 21 days!

The kitchen is your most-used room of the house, and there are a lot of different items stored in there.

If you want to see progress in your home-organization efforts, focus on one space until there is absolutely nothing else that can be decluttered or organized.

Yes, the rest of your house will feel even more unorganized as you create better organization in your kitchen, but the feeling of completion as you walk into that space will show you that you can get organized.

Learn how much time it takes to do your tasks.

Difficulty planning can make organizing hard for those dealing with ADHD—especially when it comes to the concept of time. You may find yourself putting off a 5minute task because it feels like it will take an hour, or trying to squeeze an hour-long task into 15 minutes.

When I had little kids, I always had a long legal pad to-do list where I would write down everything that I needed to do to get it out of my head and on paper. When I got really overwhelmed, I would put little numbers next to everything that was on my to-do list, like 20, 40, 60, 90, 10, 5.

One day, my mother was helping me with my children. She saw my to-do list and asked, "What are all these little numbers?"

I said, "Well, that's how long each of those tasks takes."

She was surprised and said, "Well, how do you know that that's how long each of those tasks takes?"

I said, "Well, I just know. Don't you know how long all of your tasks take?"

She said, "No."

Then I started asking my friends, "Do you know how long all of your tasks take?"

They said, "What are you talking about?" It was like I was speaking a foreign language. It was then that I realized that not everybody knows how long it takes to do even the repetitive routine tasks on their to-do lists.

Getting a better sense of how long tasks take you will help you to plan your day and increase your productivity. While this skill comes more naturally to some than others, anyone can develop it.

Problem: You don't know how long tasks take to complete.

Here's a good example: For a long time, I hated emptying the dishwasher. I don't know why. I would get it run, but I hated emptying the dishwasher because I thought it took 20 minutes.

If I was going to empty the dishwasher, I thought, "You might as well turn a TV show on." It was going to take forever.

Solution: Estimate the time each task on your to-do list will take you—and then write down both the estimate and the actual amount of time it takes next to the task. You may be pleasantly surprised to discover that some of the tasks you've been dreading take a lot less time than you thought.

One day, I thought, "Well, let's just time myself." I emptied the dishwasher at normal speed and I timed myself.

It took four minutes.

I was shocked. "It only takes four minutes to empty the dish-washer?"

Now, I empty the dishwasher every single morning. When I go to empty the dishwasher while I'm getting the kids ready for school, I look at the clock and I think, "Do I have four minutes?" Almost always, I do, and I get started.

If it's cutting it close, I think, "Hmm, it's cutting it close. I'll just do the top of the dishwasher," or I won't do it at all. But knowing that emptying the dishwasher takes four minutes allows me to squeeze that task in here and there, wherever I can fit it in.

I've learned that it takes me 20 minutes to get ready in the morning... hair, makeup, shower, the whole nine yards, 20 minutes.

When you know it takes you 20 minutes, then you know if you can hit that snooze alarm one more time, and what you have to eliminate if you do.

Avoiding making to-do lists does not make you less overwhelmed.

Problem: You are avoiding what you don't want to do. It's not even on a list.

Maybe it's because you'll be overwhelmed or it's too much, or you don't want to see how much that is. You put less on your to-do list so you're not overwhelmed. But then you forget things and end up overwhelmed anyway.

Solution: The first step is to start making one list of absolutely everything that needs to be done. When you aren't good at planning and prioritizing, it's often because you're not putting everything that needs to be done on your to-do list.

Your first to-do list can be as massive as you want, but your second to-do list will be the things that you are going to do today... and it should be able to fit on a post-it note.

Look at your first list (we'll call this your master list) and pick out two to three big tasks that you're going to do for the day.

For example, on my list, I might have "record a podcast," "go out to lunch," and "do two loads of laundry."

Wait—don't leave me! I know you are thinking...

What do you mean? My standard list is:

- Go to work
- Go to gym
- Prepare lunch and dinner (arguably two tasks)

Even skipping the gym, that's two things that need to get done pretty much every day, leaving only one open slot.

And that doesn't even begin to start in on:

- Laundry
- Grocery shopping
- Cleaning kitchen, bathroom, etc.
- Drive kids to appointments
- Go to doctors'/dentist appointments
- Help elderly neighbor with snow shoveling
- Shovel own drive
- Do taxes
- Etc.

Yes, I know. Our lives are maxed out! So here is what I have observed. We cram as much as we can on our lists, but we don't get those things crossed off.

We feel overwhelmed, unaccomplished, and depressed.

This executive function of planning is really a productivity skill more than an organizational skill. It will flourish and develop as your home and life begin to have more physical order.

My next book will dive deeper into these gigantic to-do lists we have (be looking for that resource in fall 2017). For now, just write it all down.

We need to start somewhere. And that starting place is *only* three tasks for the next day. If you work full time, go to the gym, and cook your meals, you are probably out of time. You can always add more tasks once your top three are done, but if you are tired and the day is over, you can be done.

Problem: You might not have enough time.

No joke. If you are cleaning your house (28 hours a week), earning an income (20–50 hours a week), and raising kids or taking care of family members (potentially infinite hours per week) you are out of time.

Solution: I suggest outsourcing tasks like cleaning and yard work.

I understand this is not always financially feasible. Your other option is to recognize that you may not be able to do everything you feel you "should" do, and focus on making progress in a few areas.

Putting more items on your daily to-do list will not create more time for you to get them done.

Problem: You want to get more done, so you put more on your daily to-do list.

Solution: Pick only three items to get done every day and plan them the night before.

The longer you do this, the easier it will be and the more progress you will make. You may only get three things done tomorrow, but you will get three things done!

The easiest way to create your daily list is to do it the night before. Look at your calendar for the next day and pick two or three big things to get done tomorrow.

Pick a time of day you are going to do each task, and write down how long you think it is going to take.

Sometimes the timing of your tasks may get moved around, but your post-it note will keep you focused on what you want to get done that day.

According to Brian Tracy, for every minute you spend planning, you save up to 10 minutes in execution.[2]

---

2   Brian Tracy, "Plan Ahead and Increase Productivity," *Brian Tracy International* (blog), http://www.briantracy.com/blog/time-management/plan-ahead-and-increase-productivity/.

No kidding. If you spend 12 minutes planning your day, you can save yourself 2 hours the next day. If you don't believe me, try it.

Start the night before, when you go to bed. If you're not used to doing this, think about your day, think about what you have going on the next day, and plan the two to three things that you're going to get done the next day.

Just start with that. The next day, those things will be on your mind. But here's what I find happens. I've never read this anywhere, but I know it's true. My brain actually works on my to-do list while I'm sleeping. It's awesome.

When I decide what the two to three things are that I'm going to do tomorrow, all night long my brain is working on the items on my list. When I wake up, my thoughts are much more together and fluid, and I am ready to tackle the day.

Action steps for improving your planning as it relates to home organization:

1. **Learn how long different tasks take you.** Maybe it's 10 minutes to change the laundry, 4 minutes to unload the dishwasher, an hour to go through the Sunday Basket, 15 minutes to put away all the laundry, 7 minutes to empty and take out the trash.

   Knowing these numbers will be the key to getting more out of each day.

2. **Have only... place you list all your to-do items.** Keeping all your "to-do"s on one master list will help you get more done, because you will have a place to write down all of your ideas.

3. **Plan your top three tasks for each day the night before**. Every night, pick the top three tasks you will do tomorrow and estimate how long they will take. Then, the next day, write down how long each task actually took.

Related Organize 365 podcast episodes

• Episode 62 – How to Create Morning and Evening Routines

• Episode 116 – Monthly & Yearly Checklists

• Episode 60 – Sunday Basket® Planning Printables (Weekly Planning)

• Episode 65 – 10 Ways to Outsource Your Household Tasks

• Episode 128 – How to Hire Household Help

Executive Function #6: Organization

What is the executive function of organization?

When people hear the word "organization," they usually think of the organization of materials. That's the ability to impose order on work, play, and storage spaces.

The executive function of organization is related: it means keeping track of things. Not necessarily organizing a space, but your ability to remember things—what they are and where they are.

It's funny that I'm tackling the executive skill of organization last, but you can see how organization is more than just one thing, right?

Here is why you need the executive function of organization to get your home organized.

Having one place for your items, knowing where that place is and returning items to that place are essential for maintaining organization in your home.

The executive skill of organization is more about putting things away than creating new organizing projects and cute labels for your stuff. It is the discipline of cleaning up after yourself.

Give everything a home.

Problem: You don't put things away, because you never defined where "away" was.

The number one mistake I see being made over and over by people who struggle in this area is that they keep trying different systems.

Your disorganization is not related to how trendy your organizational system is or whether your drawer could be photographed for a magazine.

Change is your enemy. New is not better!

Solution: Keeping your keys in the same boring spot for 20 years is *perfect*!

Once you find something that works, *keep* it!

Organizing your home is not where you need to show off your creative side. Save that for your clothes, decorating, and passion projects.

Home organization should be functional first.

Organize your passion projects last.

Everyone has 1–3 current passion projects. Passion projects are hobbies, memory items, or pursuits that we identify with and that make us come alive. We overbuy and overcollect in these areas because our desire to know and do more is unquenchable.

My passion projects include traditional photo albums and my business.

Passion projects are not necessarily a monetary investment. But they are always a huge emotional and time investment.

Problem: Because we are so passionate and invested in our hobbies, we naturally want to get those organized first... which is always a bad idea.

We don't want to get rid of anything, so we circle around and around, making neater stacks of pieces and parts while making no progress.

Passion projects are hard to explain to others. We do not have a rational reason why we are saving what we are saving, but we know we "need" to keep it.

I am totally cool with that, but over time, I want you to get down to 1–3 passion projects. You can't be passionate about everything.

You can learn more about Passion Projects in the Organize 365 Podcast #126

Solution: Identify 1–3 passions for each family member. Next, focus on *non-passion* areas of clutter while relocating any passion-project items to one space or one room in the home.

No one is passionate about everything. Once you have your passion projects defined, move on to decluttering and organizing the areas of your home that are functional.

Reduce the quantity of items you keep.

Problem: You have too much stuff.

Sorry.

Solution: It is just easier to keep track of less stuff. Keep everything you want in your passion area (cooking, crafting, animals, etc.), and reduce the amount you have everywhere else in your house.

The less stuff you have, the easier it is to find stuff. The whole process of decluttering and getting your house organized involves getting rid of the stuff that you don't need. Because the less stuff you have, the easier it is going to be to find the things you need.

Your home will naturally accumulate more and more each day as you bring in purchases, mail, and groceries. Decluttering—getting rid of junk mail, old food, and items that are no longer useful—needs to be a weekly occurrence as well.

Set up a donation box in your laundry room, front hall closet, or garage, and get in the habit of taking items you no longer use or need to the box right away.

Put things away!

Problem: No one wants to put things away. Not even organized people. They do it because they like knowing where things are, and they enjoy an uncluttered and organized space more than they dislike picking up after themselves.

Solution: Set aside time every day to pick up and put away your items.

Remember preschool? The teacher would start playing the pick-up-your-toys music and everyone would stop playing and start cleaning?

Afterward, she would read you a story or you had a snack before you went home. The next morning, the room was clean and you were ready for a new day of play.

How about when you were a teenager and your mom wouldn't let you go out on the weekend until your room was clean? You grumbled and complained, but when you were done, it felt great to walk back into that clean room.

When was the last time you felt that feeling?

Knowing "it" was clean and organized?

"It" could be…

- Your house
- Your kitchen
- Your closet
- Your car
- Your purse

Awhile, huh?

I know. It's okay.

You will get there. But this time… clean up after you are done playing, and don't go out until you pick up your closet.

You have a choice.

I know you feel out of control, but you have a choice.

You can change the way you feel and the environment you are in.

You can.

No, it is never going to be perfect.

Yes, it is going to be an investment of time and energy. But it's worth it.

I was a preschool teacher. I loved teaching children how to put away their toys. They felt empowered when they did it right.

I am a mom of teenagers with ADHD. Helping them learn how to clean and maintain their bedrooms was a challenge. It wasn't easy. It took years.

None of that matters when I hear the vacuum cleaner on a Saturday morning and a chipper teen saying they are ready to go to the mall and… *yes*! Their room is clean!

That discipline and skill did not come easily to them, but it is now a way of life that will serve them long into their adult lives.

Organization is not a skill you are born with. It is a skill that you develop over time. And *yes*! You can become organized, but you will need to work at it.

Action steps for improving your organization of your stuff as it relates to home organization:

1. **Give everything a home.** Pick a place to lay your keys overnight and use the same place for the next 20 years!
2. **Organize your passion projects last.** Define each family member's passion projects and where they will live. Then

set out to organize everything else. Reduce the quantity of items you keep in every area that is not a passion for you.

3. **Take time to put your things away.** Straighten up the kitchen daily. Go through the main living areas weekly. Once you get a space organized, set aside a few minutes a day to keep the area maintained.

Related Organize 365 podcast episodes

• Episode 126 – 5 Reasons Why to Organize Your Passion Projects LAST

CONCLUSION

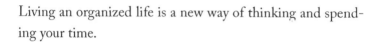

Living an organized life is a new way of thinking and spending your time.

As you read this book, I am sure there were many times where you thought, "I don't have time for this."

I know.

I agree with you. To change your life from disorganized to organized is a seismic shift.

This little book packs a big punch in changing your mindset about organization.

Understanding how each of the executive functions of the mind impacts home organization gives you power to take back your home and move from cluttered to organized.

Here's the good news. The change happens in your mind first. Just the fact that you have a new understanding of how your brain works will impact your organization without you lifting a finger.

I believe everyone *can* become organized.

Yes, you too.

Organization is a learnable skill. Understanding your unique strengths and weaknesses will help you make quicker, longer-lasting progress in your home-organization journey.

I *know* you can do this!

I'm here to help.

Listen to the weekly podcast for more inspiration and motivation to take back home!

☺
Lisa

Part 3

RESOURCES

THE SUNDAY BASKET

(FROM THE MINDSET OF ORGANIZATION: TAKE BACK YOUR HOUSE ONE PHASE AT A TIME)

The Sunday Basket was the system I created to help me get on top of all the paper and daily "todo"s I had as an adult.

Everything starts with the Sunday Basket. I didn't realize it when I started the system years ago, but pretty much everything I know about organizing can be learned with the Sunday Basket. You will learn prioritization, as well as how to deal with mail, projects, and reference items.

It's a big deal to make a Sunday Basket. It usually takes ten hours to get everything together and done the first time. After that, the Sunday Basket becomes a tool that you will use week after week. It usually takes people about six weeks to get into the flow of using a Sunday Basket.

Some of you may be thinking, "Ugh, a basket, I don't even like baskets. That's so 1980s!" So before I go any further, I'll admit that, yes, I'm a country 1980s kind of girl. But your Sunday Basket could be a box or a bag. I don't care. Just get some kind of container that you're going to use to collect all of the mail and papers that come into your life.

You will check this container on a regular basis. I check mine on Sunday… that's why I call it the Sunday Basket. It may be a Friday box for you or a Tuesday bag or whatever you want it to be, but it has to have a day and it has to be a container for paper.

Step 1 – Find all of your paper.

And I mean all of your paper. Your first basket is going to be one or two laundry baskets.

Grab a laundry basket and go on a scavenger hunt all around the house. You're going to pick up all of that paper that needs to be processed, like the mail you left in the car, or the stuff you left in the garage on the way into the house. You'll search your laundry room, the counter by the bathtub, that space near your dresser. You'll look in the kitchen and on the dining room table.

Maybe you put something down when you went into the kids' room to tuck them into bed. You'll probably find paper everywhere: mail, catalogs, bills, forms to fill out, things that need to be filed, things that need to be shredded, all of it.

I don't want you to do anything with your paper. You're not processing it or taking any action whatsoever. You're just containerizing it all into laundry baskets.

If you fill two laundry baskets and there is still more paper in your house that needs to be processed, I want you to stop and do this process with two laundry baskets full of paper. Then start over again. Some people have lived in their houses for decades, and honestly, they could easily fill ten to twelve laundry baskets. I am not making any judgments. This is just a process of how to tackle it.

You may be thinking, "I need an accountant and a bulldozer. That's what I need."

No, you don't. You can do this. Just fill one laundry basket at a time. Do this entire system, adding another laundry basket and another. You didn't get into this situation overnight, and you're not going to get out of it overnight. We just have to start somewhere or we're always going to be living in the piles of paper.

On average, people fill two laundry baskets.

You might think, "She's crazy, I won't even have one laundry basket full of paper." But when you really start picking up all the magazines, catalogs, newspapers, and kids' school papers, you'll have two laundry baskets. Then you'll be thinking, "Oh, my gosh, two laundry baskets. I cannot believe I have two laundry baskets' worth of papers that need to be processed."

Finding your paper does two things. First, it gets the paper out of all the other rooms of your house. Now, everywhere you go, you're not going to see paper. That will bring down your stress level and give you some breathing space.

Second, when you put all your paper in those laundry baskets, you will know where to look for things. When you find out that you were supposed to send in a permission slip, that's okay. It's somewhere in those two laundry baskets. It may take you fifteen minutes to find it, but it's not going to take you an hour and a half.

When you don't have a Sunday Basket, you have to look in your car, in the garage, and in every single room in your house to find that piece of paper. The beauty of the Sunday Basket is that all your paper is in one place and all you have to do is start going through that basket.

Step 2—Separate the active paper from the archive papers.

Make yourself a nice cup of coffee or a glass of wine. Turn on mindless TV in the background, if that's what you like, or some nice upbeat music that's going to keep you energized. Sit down with your laundry basket.

Breathe.

Get another empty laundry basket and a trash can (or recycling bin). As you pull each piece of paper out of the laundry basket, you are going to divide them into piles.

1. If it's trash, just trash it.
2. Paper like insurance statements, tax returns, or the kids' report cards—anything you want to keep and file—goes in a to-file pile. They're a long-term item you want to keep, but they don't require any action.
3. We are not going to file those now. Make a big pile of everything that needs to be filed, and then take that pile to wherever the filing cabinet is and put it there.
4. Make a pile of anything that needs to be shredded.

These three steps are going to get rid of anywhere from 60-80 percent of your papers in that laundry basket.

The only items left in your laundry basket are active papers... like the invitation to that graduation party you need to reply to and buy a gift for, the permission slips that need to go back to school, the bills that need to be paid, the email you printed out about the dates for the kids' summer camp that you need to add to the Google calendar, the Post-it note that's in there to remind you to buy a Father's Day gift for your dad. All of those things are what you now have left in the Sunday Basket. They are all actionable items.

Step 3—Work on the actionable items in your basket.

Your Sunday Basket is all about items that we need to make decisions on or do something with.

The Sunday Basket only works if you set aside time in your calendar to do the Sunday Basket activities weekly. I'll be honest, some weeks that's two hours. Other weeks, I can get the Sunday Basket done in fifteen minutes.

Fifteen minutes, two hours, it doesn't matter. You need some time to go through this basket every week.

The first thing you're going to do is to take every single thing out of the basket and put those papers in a pile on the floor. Your basket should be empty.

Pick up every single piece of paper and say to yourself, "Can this wait until next Sunday?" If you're just starting out, or you're in a really busy phase of life, you're going to want to defer as many decisions as you can and put the papers back in the Sunday Basket.

There are two reasons for this. First, you do not want a lot on your to-do list, and second, the more you defer things week after week, the more often you actually decide not to do them at all. Fifty percent of your actionable Sunday Basket items never get done and you will decide to recycle or shred them.

For example, we have Time Warner Cable. I needed to get digital adapter boxes for each of our TVs in order for them to receive digital cable a year from now. I kept putting that letter back in my Sunday Basket for probably two months before I finally called them and had the digital adapters sent to me.

When the digital adapters arrived, I took the actual boxes that were sent to me and I put those in my Sunday Basket. Then, I kept deferring the task of setting them up for about a month.

So, in addition to paper, you may have physical items in your Sunday Basket.

Any household projects that need to be done are going to end up in your Sunday Basket. And what a great place for them, right? Every week, you get to decide, Is this the week I'm going to plant the vegetable garden? Is this the week we're going to call the guy to paint the house or to get new gutters? If the actual project does not fit in the Sunday Basket, put a note in the Sunday Basket to remind you.

As you go through the Sunday Basket process, you will start to think, "Okay, nope. I'm not doing the Time Warner Cable project. Yes, I need to pay this bill. No, I don't need to pay that bill. Yes, we need to fill out this form. No, we don't need to fill out that form."

At the end of each session, you will have things in your Sunday Basket that will sit there until next Sunday for you. And you'll have a handful of things that are sitting in your lap or on the kitchen counter, things that you need to act on and do, either today or sometime this week.

Step 4—Group like items together.

I particularly like slash pocket folders for this. Slash pocket folders are three-hole-punched plastic folders that are sold in the binder supply section of the store. Sometimes they have tabs on them, sometimes they don't. You can get them in clear, but usually you'll find them in assorted colors.

Slash pocket folders are how I organize the papers in my Sunday Basket.

After you have used your Sunday Basket for about four to six weeks, you're going to start thinking, "Oh, my gosh. I know that I have to plan the VBS camp in August, but it is May, and every single Sunday, I'm going through and I'm touching eighteen different pieces of paper because I'm coordinating Vacation Bible School. Touching each of these pieces is driving me crazy."

Or, "We are going to go on vacation to Florida, and I have twelve pieces of paper that go with that." Or, "The kids don't go back to school until September first, but I'm collecting all these papers I need to keep track of until August first."

These are natural groupings of paper. What you need is a VBS folder, a first-day-at-school folder, and a going-to-Florida-vacation folder.

You don't want to start with slash pocket folders. Your paper, not your goals, will determine what your folders should be. If you do it the other way around, then you'll start thinking, "What would be the ideal folders?" There are no ideal folders. It's not a filing system. It's just a nice way to keep papers, little notes, and projects together.

Once you have these like items grouped together, it becomes much quicker to go through the Sunday Basket because instead of having to look at all of the papers that go with your vacation, you just need to look at the folder that says "Florida Vacation" and ask yourself, "Can this wait until next Sunday?" You might say, "Yeah, we're not leaving yet. I'll just add in all these little notes, or I'll rewrite my list, put it in there, and then put it back in the Sunday Basket. I don't need that folder out." Maybe the next folder is "Summer Tutoring." You might think, "Yeah, we need to keep that one out. I need to schedule that and talk to the teachers."

Creating your Sunday Basket is Organization 101

Before you jump into The Productive Home Solution™, organizing ALL your papers, or working on your productivity, I want you to have a Sunday Basket. When you start organizing, it always gets more chaotic before it gets organized, right?

How many times have you started an organization project and had someone walk in and say, "You're organizing it? It looks like you're blowing it up."

Or sometimes you have to leave to take the kids to a doctor in the middle of that organizational blowup and you don't even get back to it for three or four days. Then, you're living in even *more* chaos before you can get organized, right?

There are a couple of things that you need to do to set yourself up for success before you try to organize your whole house. Start with a Sunday Basket. Then, it doesn't matter if you're in the middle of organizing your closet and there are clothes everywhere and you can barely even walk through your bedroom. If your kid comes in and says, "Mrs. So-and-so needs that paper back," you can go straight downstairs, find the Sunday Basket, find that piece of paper, sign it, and give it to the kid. It takes maybe fifteen minutes.

If you don't have a Sunday Basket, this is what happens. You say, "Oh, my gosh. I can't believe I took time for myself to organize my closet. I'm not being a good mother. I don't even know where these papers are. Who am I to think I can get organized? This is insane. I need to just stop. I don't even know if I can do this."

I know because this is what I would think.

But if you can stop, go find that paper, and get back to what you're doing, you think, "This is great. I know where the important papers are, and I know where the bills are. I'm going to handle that every Sunday. It's okay for me to prioritize organizing my closet. I may not be organized yet, but I'm on my way, and I know where all the important papers are for our family while I do this for me."

Then, yes, it's okay. Let the laundry and the dishes pile up. Your house will not implode if you take two or three days to organize your master closet or if you take a couple hours a day for the 100 Day Home Organization Program so that your house functions better. You need to have one place... only one place... where all of those kinds of papers go. And then, one time a week when you check it so you can stay on top of those requests and be the awesome, organized woman that you are.

You can download the Sunday Basket Quick Guide, SHRED Printable, and How to Sort Paper Printables at www.organize365.com/book-bonus.

The Productive Home Solution™ Program

The Productive Home Solution™ is the next step in your home organization journey. The Productive Home Solution™ is a year-long curated & detailed home organization program, designed to get your home organized in the most logical order without the organization being undone as you move from space to space.

Take the Organize 365 Productive CEO quiz online and pinpoint your "why" for getting organized, nail down how much time you can commit to getting organized, and discover where you are in the declutter/organize/productivity cycle. You can find the quiz for free at organize365.com/quiz.

According to a Boston Marketing Firm, the average American wastes fifty-five minutes a day looking for things they own but can't find.[3] Spend the time upfront and organize your home so that you do not spend it looking for things instead.

While I designed the program to be completed in as little as fifteen minutes a day, let's be honest. The real reason people

---

3 *Newsweek* (June 7, 2004)

want a fifteen-minute-a-day challenge is that they are overwhelmed, exhausted, and scared.

Overwhelmed at:

- the disorganized state of their home
- the energy it will take to do it all
- the idea of learning a different way of doing things

Exhausted from:

- daily life
- looking for things and frustrated that they cannot find them
- living this way

Scared:

- that it works for everyone else, but it will not work for them
- that they will pay for the course, but not take the action
- that by committing to this challenge they have to change

What I have found is that the time limits fade once you see results.

Time and time again, our clients keep organizing when we leave their homes at night. And once you decide it is time to get organized, you are going to be staying up late and gleefully organizing on the weekends, too. I know it sounds hard to believe, but it is true. You will because it is not about the amount of time you have.

Once you see that this works and you can do it, you will be empowered. You will start to look forward to making the decisions about where your stuff goes instead of living in the exhaustion and stress of your stuff telling you how to feel.

It is not all rosy.

As you can tell, I am an optimist. I am one of those "always happy even on rainy days" kind of people. But getting your whole home organized is hard, and it does take time to dig yourself out of the chaos.

Once you buy this membership, you have lifetime access. You can do the program as many times as you want. Your membership will never expire. You have access to all of the materials from the first day, and you can work at your own pace.

The first three to four weeks will be rough. Your inner voice will make up reasons why you lack the time, energy, or skills to do this, but you don't! And the mess will talk back to you, too. You will feel like you should be making more progress, faster.

But then it will happen. After Day 22, you will walk into your kitchen and it will be organized! And on Day 40, your primary bedroom, bath, closet, and accessories will all be completed as well. This will give you the power to move on to your books and office area.

I also want to give you a fair warning. Even though this is a year-long program, I needed to do the program three times before my home felt really organized. I recommend that everyone plan to work through the program three times and allow at least one full year for your home to get fully organized. Decluttering during different seasons of the year helps you to see if you really *should* keep that turkey roasting pan and the camping tent. I have observed that most people can only declutter around 30 percent of their belongings at a time. Going back through the same parts of your home three times helps you to continue to analyze and get to the right amount of stuff for you.

So, if you are READY for a change, go to Organize365.com and see our most current offering in The Productive Home Solution.

I look forward to helping *you* get organized!

ELECTRONIC RESOURCES

This section is written by Betsy Fuller, MS, CCC-SLP. Betsy is the CEO of Communication Circles, a unique agency that provides consulting services to app developers and tech companies, as well as direct services to people with disabilities utilizing tech solutions.

For more information about Betsy and to view her services, go to www.communicationcircles.com.

Apps and mobile devices like iPads and smartphones can make a tremendous difference in the lives of people with ADHD and other conditions that create difficulties with executive functioning.

For people with these challenges, trying to be organized and writing things down is often frustrating. You may find yourself writing hundreds of sticky notes: lists, phone numbers, names, and dates. If one blows away in a big wind or ends up crumpled in the bottom of your purse, it—and all the information on it—is gone! When you use your phone or tablet to keep these little pieces of information together, you know where they all are and you can have them with you at all times. If you sync the apps (and therefore your information) across all your devices, it is even better! I often use the Notes app on my phone to record quick pieces of information I need to remember. Once synced, anything I write in the Notes app on my phone also shows up in the Notes app on my iPads and on my MacBook. It is magical!

There are some apps that work across platforms, meaning they can be used on any combination of device operating systems (iOS, Android, Windows). Look for these apps if you use a variety of devices. The devices I use on a regular basis are all Apple/iOS, so I stick with apps in the Apple App Store. (iPads and iPhones are iOS devices.)

Tens of thousands of apps are available in the Apple App Store, in Google Play, and in the Windows Store. Trying to find the apps you need can feel overwhelming, so I am going to tell you about a few apps that can change your life through better organization.

NOTE-TAKING AND LIST APPS

Apps that help you build lists or take notes are priceless! If you have trouble remembering what you need to do or keeping track of items you have or need, a note-taking or list app can be a lifesaver.

When looking at note-taking and list apps, look for these features:

Flexible List Types–What type of list do you like? Do you want to check off items when they are done or erase them? Do you want each entry date-stamped?

- *Auto-Archive Feature*–This feature saves a backup of your notes or lists.
- *Delete Protection*–How difficult is it to accidentally erase an entry? You don't want to accidentally delete your notes or lists!
- *Synchronization*–Can you sync across all your devices? I like apps I can use on my Mac, iPhone, and iPads. If you have a PC, an iPhone, and an Android tablet, consider apps that can be used on multiple devices and operating systems.
- *Sharing*–Can you share your list with someone else? It is nice to be able to share a list or a note with a co-worker or a family member. This feature is especially helpful for shopping or packing lists.
- *Location Reminders*–Apps with this functionality will send you an alert when you enter or leave a predefined area.

- *Color Coding*–The ability to set different colors for each person, task, or priority can be very helpful.

Recommended Apps:

Orderly–To-Do Lists, Location-Based Reminders by Tekton Technologies (P) Ltd.

Available for iOS.

This app is very visual. You can create cards for each task list and prioritize them. You can set a time and date deadline or a location reminder for each task. You can also add recurring tasks and set reminders for them. Entries are searchable.

Notes by Apple

Preinstalled on all Apple devices.

Notes is a staple in my life! I jot down ideas on the Notes app daily. The app allows you to add typed notes as well as handwritten ones. You can also attach web links and photos. The app also has a list-building feature that inserts checkboxes. You can share a note, and the person you share with can edit the note. You can also send your note via email, text message, Twitter, Facebook, Voxer, WhatsApp, LinkedIn, Trello, and more. The notes are searchable, too!

Reminders by Apple

Preinstalled on all Apple devices.

Reminders allows you to make lists, set reminders, and share these items with others. You can also set location-based reminders with this app.

NINE–A Visual To-Do and Reminder List by Ideas Made Digital

Available for iOS.

NINE is a photo-based list app, meaning you take photos to make your list. Each photo is then paired with text and put into an icon-based list. You can add a date and/or time-based reminder; recurring reminders are also supported. The app automatically adds a location to your entry. You can send your entries to other people via text message, email, Voxer, WhatsApp, Twitter, Facebook, and more. You can also copy your entries into the Reminders app, the Notes app, Google Drive, Asana, and other programs.

Cozi Family Organizer by Cozi, Inc.

Available for Android, iOS, Windows, and at cozi.com.

Cozi is a very robust app that includes to-do lists, shopping lists, a recipe and meal planner, and a family journal. It is easily shareable with its family sharing feature. Our family uses the Cozi app for all our grocery lists. I add items to the grocery list, and my husband can then open the app on his phone and see my list while he is shopping. I use the to-do lists for all my packing lists. I can check off items as I go and then clear the checkmarks to use the list for a subsequent trip. The calendar feature on this app can be used with other online calendars such as Google Calendar, Apple Calendar, Outlook, Yahoo Calendar, and Windows Live. Cozi is a great tool, but because it is so feature-rich, it can be confusing for some people.

Evernote by Evernote Corporation

Available for Android, iOS, Windows, and at evernote.com.

Evernote is also web-based, so it can be used on a Mac or PC computer. Like Cozi, this app is very feature-rich. I had to watch some YouTube tutorial videos to feel comfortable using it. However, once you learn to use the features, it is life changing! Evernote saves notes. The notes can take the form of a to-do list, a reminder, a photo of a sketch, or a photo of a handwritten note. Notes can be tagged and stored within folders in the app. You can also save webpages within Evernote. Evernote allows you to email notes to the app—even forwarded emails. Everything is searchable once it is in the app. Anything stored in the app is immediately accessible via all devices with Evernote installed.

CALENDARS

It is difficult to switch from a paper calendar to an online calendar, but it is so worth it! Having all your appointments on your phone ensures you always have your calendar with you. Online calendars can be color-coded so you can see at a glance if an appointment is for you, your spouse, or your children. You can also color-code items in your calendar as reminders for future events. Many online calendars are sharable as well. I use a shared Google calendar with my administrative assistant so she can schedule appointments for me. I can then sync that shared Google Calendar with iCal on my iPhone, and I can see what she has scheduled for me.

I made the switch to an online calendar slowly. Initially, I used a Google Calendar and I printed it out. Every week, I would print the online calendar so I had a piece of paper to touch and write on. This was a good method for me to make the switch gradually and painlessly. At the end of the week, I transferred anything I wrote on the printed version of the calendar onto the online version and then printed the next week. I now only use an online calendar, and I haven't looked back!

Here are some features to look for in a calendar app:

- *Sharing*–Is the calendar sharable? It is helpful to be able to share your calendar with your family members and other important people in your life.

- *Color Coding*–Can you color-code the entries in the calendar? I have a color for each person in our family, and this color scheme is consistent through all our calendars, our paper filing system, and even extends to actual objects we own! For example, I am pink, my older son is blue, my younger son is green, and my husband is white or black. I also color-code various aspects of my business. The nonprofit I consult with is coded in orange; my business appointments are all in purple.
- *Locations*–Can you include the locations of appointments? Do you need a calendar that will link to a map or driving directions app?
- *Reminders*–Can you set reminders for appointments? Can the app notify you with the frequency you desire?
- *Recurring Appointments*–Can you set recurring appointments? Will the app repeat these appointments as often as you need?

Recommended Apps:

iCal by Apple

Preinstalled on all Apple devices.

iCal allows you to share appointments and is compatible with other calendars, such as Google Calendar, for sharing. iCal also offers a color-coding feature. Within iCal, you can set locations, reminders, and recurring appointment times.

Cozi Family Organizer by Cozi, Inc.

Available for Android, iOS, Windows, and at cozi.com.

Cozi's calendar offers color coding and can be shared. It also allows you to look at a daily view of color-coded events. Gold members can see a monthly view as well. The calendar feature on this app can be used with other online calendars such as Google Calendar, Apple Calendar, Microsoft Outlook, Yahoo Calendar, and Windows Live.

Google Calendar by Google, Inc.

Available for Android, iOS, and at google.com.

Google Calendar allows for color coding and sharing.

Timers

Timers are extremely helpful, and having a timer at your fingertips can encourage its use. We often need encouragement to focus. If you plan to work, write, meditate, or exercise for a certain number of minutes, it is easier to get through the task without becoming distracted if you set a timer.

Recommended Apps:

Clock on Your Device

The built-in clock on your phone should have a timer function. On the iPhone, you can set the buzzer for a variety of different sounds, including songs that you own through iTunes.

Time Timer by Time Timer LLC

Available for Android and iOS.

Time Timer is a great timer app for kids or adults who need a visual timer. This app is based on a physical product (also called the Time Timer) that has been used in classrooms for years. The app shows a visual representation of an analog clock face. As the timer counts down, color fills the clock face; the minutes remaining are indicated in white. The app is customizable and timers can be saved and reused.

GRAPHIC ORGANIZERS

Graphic organizers allow students—or anyone doing any writing—to organize their thoughts. Using a graphic organizer, you can enter all of your information for your writing within a visual organizer. Some graphic-organizer apps allow you to make an outline, too.

Recommended Apps:

Popplet by Notion

Available for iOS and at popplet.com.

Popplet is a mind-mapping app that allows you to make graphic organizers that help you write out your thoughts. Popplet allows you to make your own graphic organizers without preset templates. You can color-code templates and add text, photos, and handwriting or drawings.

Inspiration Maps VPP by Inspiration Software, Inc.

Available for iOS.

Inspiration Maps was originally software for a computer. It is a great mind-mapping/graphic-organizer app that helps you get your thoughts from your head onto paper. The paid version has many templates to choose from. After completing a template, you push one button and all of the information you entered on the template becomes an outline. This app is great if you need to organize your thoughts into words for blog posts, papers for classes, or emails. Children in second grade or above will also benefit from it.

VISUAL SCHEDULES

Visual schedules are very, very helpful for disorganized kids, children who have difficulty with transitions, and kids who need firm boundaries. By using an app for a visual schedule, you can carry the schedule with you and quickly make a new schedule or make changes to an existing schedule. Paper visual schedules are time consuming to make. You must find the pictures, print them, cut them, laminate them, and then use Velcro to place them on a schedule strip. You also must plan ahead to make sure you have all the cards you might need for the visual schedule. By using a virtual schedule on a tablet or phone, you eliminate these barriers.

Recommended Apps:

First Then Visual Schedule by Good Karma

Applications, Inc.

Available on Android and iOS.

This visual scheduling app allows you to make custom visual schedules. In addition to photos and text that can be moved or marked complete, you can also add video to the schedules. The app also allows you to set timers.

ChoiceWorks by Bee Visual, LLC

Available on iOS.

ChoiceWorks is a visual scheduling app that also has content to help children with waiting and learning about feelings. The app is customizable.

MEDICAL APPS

Your smartphone and tablet can also help you organize your medical information. Don't overlook this important aspect of personal information management. Keeping medical records organized can literally save your life. When you need to gather your records and share them with new doctors, CareSync is the best app on the market. Other medical apps can keep you healthy and protect you in case of an emergency.

Recommended Apps:

Health by Apple

Preinstalled on all Apple devices.

Make sure you complete your medical profile in the built-in Health app. It is accessible by emergency responders even if your phone is locked.

CareSync by CareSync, Inc.

Available on Android, iOS, and at caresync.com.

CareSync is a great app that helps you organize your family's medical records. The app is free, but I pay for some of the premium features to manage my son's medical information. The paid version allows CareSync to gather, summarize, and organize records and make these records accessible from any device or from a computer. My son has a life-threatening medical condition and has been hospitalized over 100 times.

It is vital he has his medical history and records with him at all times. He's now in college and living in a dorm; CareSync has allowed him to be this independent! He simply pulls up the app and hands it to the EMTs or doctor, and they are able to treat him appropriately. The app also stores medication names and dosages and has a medication reminder feature. All the records are searchable and are arranged in an easy-to-read timeline.

SleepCycle Alarm Clock by Northcube AB

Available on <u>Android</u> and <u>iOS</u>.

Sleep Cycle is an alarm clock app that also tracks your sleep patterns and quality of sleep. You set the alarm for an approximate time you need to wake up. The alarm wakes you up when you are in a light sleep so it is easier to wake up.

FINANCIAL APPS

Keeping track of your budget and due dates of bills is hard when you are trying to keep track of it all on paper. Apps can help so much with the organization of your finances. Many banks and credit unions have their own apps; these allow you to keep an eye on your checking and savings accounts. In many cases, you can also deposit checks using your phone and the app.

Recommended Apps:

EveryDollar by The Lampo Group Incorporated

Available on Android, iOS, and at everydollar.com.

EveryDollar uses Dave Ramsey's principles to help you organize your finances, create a budget, and save money. It is very easy to use, and it is quick to set up.

Mint: Personal Finance, Budget, Bills & Money by Intuit, Inc.

Available on Android, iOS, and at mint.com.

Mint is a more complex app that syncs with multiple bank accounts and allows you to track income, spending, and saving.

MESSAGING APPS

To keep track of my conversations, I use specific messaging apps for specific people. For example, I use Voxer to communicate with my business coach and my administrative assistant. I can easily find their messages if needed. I use WhatsApp to communicate with my husband and neighbor. I know those messages will be personal and not business related.

Recommended Apps:

WhatsApp Messenger by WhatsApp Inc.

Available on Android, iOS, and Windows.

WhatsApp provides the ability to send text messages, send voice messages, and make long distance calls (no charge). It is easy to download and start using.

Voxer Walkie Talkie Messenger by Voxer LLC

Available on Android, iOS, and at voxer.com.

Voxer is like a walkie-talkie. The app can also record voice messages so you can play them back later. You can send text messages within the app.

Email Management

Organization of email is an ongoing struggle for me! Two email management tools have helped me get my email more organized so I can find emails I need and eliminate emails I do not need.

Recommended Apps:

Unroll.Me by Unroll.Me

Available on iOS or at unroll.me.

I often subscribe to emails from a company I am interested in getting information or coupons from. My email inbox gets full of those promotional emails, and I cannot find the emails I actually need. Unroll.me separates these emails and allows you to filter certain types of email or unsubscribe from mailing lists so you do not get any emails from a company in the future.

SaneBox by SaneBox

Available on iOS or at sanebox.com.

SaneBox separates your email into different folders. I use it to automatically divide my email into folders for different projects. It also prioritizes emails that are kept in the Inbox. If I am in a hurry, I can glance only at the Inbox.

By organizing your life on your phone or tablet, you will always have access to your information. I love being able to travel with just my iPad and iPhone. I know I can access my calendar and all my notes, as well as any documents I have stored in the cloud. I hope you all come to enjoy and benefit from technology as much as I do!

ABOUT THE AUTHOR

Lisa Woodruff is a productivity specialist, home organization expert, and founder and CEO of Organize 365. Lisa provides physical and motivational resources teaching busy women to take back control of their lives with functional systems that work.

She's the host of the top-rated Organize 365 Podcast, which was featured as the Woman's Day podcast of the month. She shares strategies for reducing overwhelming thoughts, clearing mental clutter, and living a productive and organized life.

Lisa has authored several Amazon bestselling books and is a sought-after trainer and speaker, often quoted as saying "Done is better than perfect" and "Progress over perfection." Her sensible and doable organizing tasks appeal to multiple generations, and her candor and relatable style make you feel as though she is right there beside you, helping you get organized as you laugh and cry together.

As a recognized thought leader, Lisa's work has been featured in many national publications such as The New York Times, Fast Company, US News and World Report, Women's World, Ladies Home Journal, Getting Organized, and Woman's Day magazines. She's been interviewed on over fifty podcasts, featured in more than fifty local TV segments, participated in countless online summits, and is a regular HuffPost and ADDitude magazine contributor.

Lisa is also a generational expert and specializes in unpacking common everyday scenarios with grace, reshaping your understanding of the role we play in the home today. Believing that organization is not a skill you're born with, but rather one that is developed over time and which changes with each season of life, she made it her mission to redefine what it means to be a woman in the home.

Lisa lives in Cincinnati with her husband, Greg, and their children, Joey and Abby.